THE SUN DANCES

PRAYERS AND BLESSINGS
FROM THE GAELIC

THE SUN DANCES

*Prayers and Blessings
from the Gaelic*

Collected and translated by
ALEXANDER CARMICHAEL

Chosen and with an Introduction by
ADAM BITTLESTON

FLORIS BOOKS

The title is taken from
'Easter Sunday,' p. 98

These verses are selected from the *Carmina Gadelica*
published in six volumes between 1900 and 1961,
available in English as a single paperback volume
from Floris Books.

This arrangement first published in 1960 by
The Christian Community Press, London
This fifth reprint published in 1999
This arrangement © 1960 Floris Books,
15 Harrison Gardens, Edinburgh

British Library CIP Data available

ISBN 0-86315-503-0

Printed in Great Britain
by Cromwell Press, Trowbridge, Wilts.

CONTENTS

ACKNOWLEDGEMENTS

THESE verses are chosen from the English translations, which accompany the Gaelic originals in the *Carmina Gadelica*, by kind permission of Sir Hugh Watson, D.K.S., and of Mr A. M. Watson, the Trustees acting under the will of the late Professor James Carmichael Watson, the owners of the copyright. *Carmina Gadelica, Hymns and Incantations, with Illustrative Notes of Words, Rites and Customs Dying and Obselete*: Orally Collected in the Highlands and Islands of Scotland by Alexander Carmichael, is published by Messrs Oliver and Boyd, Tweeddale Court, Edinburgh. The first two volumes were published in 1900 and a second edition appeared in 1928, edited by Dr Carmichael's daughter, Mrs E. C. C. Watson. The third and fourth volumes were published in 1940 and 1941, edited by his grandson, Professor James Carmichael Watson. The fifth volume appeared in 1954, edited by Professor Angus Matheson; under his editorship a sixth volume, largely consisting of notes, lexical material, and indices, is intended.

The Celtic decorations were copied by Mrs Carmichael from ancient MSS. and appear here through the help of Messrs Oliver and Boyd.

The publication of this selection would not have been possible without the unfailing encouragement and practical help of Miss Aletta Adler, of Garvald School, Dolphinton, and of Mrs Catherine de Bruyne.

INTRODUCTION

ALEXANDER CARMICHAEL was born on 1st December 1832 on the island of Lismore. He was educated at Greenock and at Edinburgh, and became a civil servant. His work took him to Greenock, Dublin, Islay, Cornwall, Skye, Uist, Oban, Uist again, and finally to Edinburgh. His official position helped him at times to persuade the government departments concerned to take measures helpful for the poor – for instance to obtain from the Board of Inland Revenue the abolition of the tax on carts and on shepherds' dogs. But his main interest was in the recording of Gaelic poetry and customs, for which he had the most intimate understanding. He wrote down what was recited to him by 'men and women throughout the Highlands and Islands of Scotland, from Arran to Caithness, from Perth to St Kilda'. He was a stately, vigorous figure, in whom the gentlest kindness was soon to be recognised. Dr Kenneth MacLeod wrote of him that he had 'a beautiful mania for setting things right and for unravelling the tangles in the lives as well as in the lore of the folk'.

The words he recorded he also translated; and those learned in the Gaelic speak of the insight which he showed as a translator. But it has not yet been widely enough recognised how great his achievement was. His English renderings were not only faithful; their grandeur and power show him as one of the translators through whom a masterpiece can be reborn in a new language.

Only a part of what he collected and translated was published before his death in 1912. On St Michael's

Day 1899, when he was sixty-six, he completed the Introduction to the first two volumes of *Carmina Gadelica: Hymns and Incantations with Illustrative Notes on Words, Rites and Customs, Dying and Obsolete: Orally Collected in the Highlands and Islands of Scotland and Translated into English*. Here Gaelic original and translation face each other, and sometimes details are given of the people and places from which the originals came.

A second edition of these two volumes was published in 1928. It was prepared by Dr Carmichael's daughter, Elizabeth Catherine Carmichael, who married in 1906 Professor W. J. Watson. Mrs Watson was for many years Editor of the *Celtic Review* and she had occupied with her husband a central position in the Gaelic movement. Their son, Professor James Carmichael Watson, published two further volumes in 1940 and 1941. Celtic studies in Scotland suffered a most tragic loss by his death in March 1942 at the age of thirty-two, while serving in the Mediterranean in H.M.S. *Jaguar*. A fifth volume with two short memoirs of Professor J. C. Watson was published in 1954 under the editorship of Professor Angus Matheson.

To appreciate the fulness of Dr Carmichael's achievement and that of those who have worked on his papers, all five volumes are necessary.

*   *   *

The poems recorded by Dr Carmichael were handed down orally, without being attributed to any particular author. How old they are, it is very hard to say. Dr Carmichael himself wrote of his collection: 'It is the product of far-away thinking come down on the long stream of time. Who the thinkers and whence the stream, who can tell? Some of the hymns may have been composed within the cloistered cells of Derry and Iona, and some of the incantations among the cromlechs of Stonehenge and the standing stones of Callarnis. These poems were composed by the learned, but they have not come down through the learned, but through the unlearned.' They were felt by those who passed them on as precious and intimate possessions, which they might have hesitated to share with anyone less sensitive to their value than Dr Carmichael. Dr Kenneth MacLeod does indeed record that 'one evening, a venerable Islesman, carried out of himself for the time being, allowed Dr Carmichael to take down from him a singularly beautiful "going into sleep" rune; early next morning, the reciter travelled twenty-six miles to exact a pledge that his "little prayer" should never be allowed to appear in print. "Think ye," said the old man, "if I slept a wink last night for thinking of what I had given away. Proud indeed shall I be if it give pleasure to yourself, but I should not like cold eyes to read it in a book." In the writer's presence, the manuscript was handed over to the reciter to be burnt there and then.'

Never in Dr Carmichael's work is there any hint of superiority towards any of the thoughts or feelings which he met among the islanders, and in their poetry – even where his contemporaries would be readiest, with grave self-satisfaction, to speak of superstition. All that belonged to the ancient life of his people seemed to him worthy of respect. He would go to endless trouble in his search for traditional poetry, often wading by dangerous sea-fords from island to island, and spending the night, after a long journey, in the open air or on a hard chair by the fireside in a shepherd's hut. He saw the treasures which he rescued in a wide perspective, and with a peculiar, humble tranquillity. It was grievous for him that so many ministers and teachers tried to stamp out Gaelic poetry and the ancient customs of the Isles. But he could admire at the same time the loyalty with which the Islanders accepted the guidance of such leaders, and himself had hatred for no man.

*　　　*　　　*

If we come unprepared to these poems, much in them may seem remote and unfamiliar. They may even be regarded as examples of 'Celtic twilight'. It has been pointed out again and again in recent years that the ancient Celts were anything but vague and misty. When they became Christians and took up the making of books, they were capable of the most complex and precise decorative art that has ever been achieved; and their narrative poetry has the qualities of clear sunlight and incisive humour. If something appears vague to us, this may be because we have difficulty in understanding and renewing what was once a very definite experience.

In those religious experiences which are of a universal kind, which are expressed in these poems, it can be seen how exact the language is.

> And grant Thou to me, Father beloved,
> From whom each thing that is freely flows,
> That no tie over-strict, no tie over-dear
>   May be between myself and this world below.

Here the right Christian middle way between asceticism and sensuality is expressed with wonderful precision. Everything good comes from God and is given freedom to be itself, to enjoy and to be enjoyed; and yet we are enslaved if we care for anything in ways that exclude the Giver. Everywhere in these poems, where at first we may have the impression that conventional sentiments are being expressed, and even unnecessarily repeated, a sensitive and subtle progress of thought is to be discovered if we are open and patient enough. Something indeed is necessarily lost in translation, and that is the music of sound in which repetition and variation plays a great part. Even *looking* at the Gaelic without being able to read or pronounce it, we can get some impression of this. For example, the first verse of 'The Lullaby of the Snow':

> Is fuar fuar a nochd mo leaba,
> Is fuar fuar a nochd mo leanabh,
> Is buan buan a nochd do chadal,
> Mis am anart 's tus am achlais.

Greater difficulty may be found where, in the poems, beings are spoken of or addressed, of whom a great part of humanity has forgotten even the names. Michael, Gabriel, Raphael, Uriel and others appear in these poems as messengers of the Divine, as they appear in the Old and New Testaments or in the *Apocrypha*.

The festival of Michael, the leader of angels in the battle against evil, was one of the great events of the year in the Islands, up to about the middle of the nineteenth century. He is called '*cra-gheal*', 'red-white' or light red; the red of courage, lightened by purity of soul. Gabriel, the bringer of the Annunciation to Mary, is also felt as very near to human beings. But so, too, are spiritual figures which are only mentioned in the Bible in books more seldom read, *Tobit* and *II Esdras*. Raphael we meet as the gentle leader of the youth Tobias, inspiring him with healing wisdom. And it is Uriel who challenges Esdras: 'Weigh me the weight of the fire, or measure me the blast of the wind, or call me again the day that is past.' He calls the human consciousness to feel its limitation, in order to approach in the right way the greatness of the spiritual world.

There was once a clearly differentiated experience behind the naming of the spiritual powers. We find this again in Goethe's *Faust*, where Raphael, Gabriel and Michael appear in the 'Prologue in Heaven'; and then, as exact knowledge, renewed in our own century in the work of Rudolf Steiner. We can indeed come to feel that religious life in our time deeply needs, in order to feel in right perspective the relationships between the earthly and the Divine, a renewed understanding of the Hierarchies, our elder brothers in the universe. For the Islanders, this was a matter of course; that man is surrounded by a multitude of spiritual beings, not so very deeply hidden in waking life, and nearer still to him in the hours of sleep. In particular, each human being has his own guardian angel, who leads and protects him in every realm, in so far as this is made possible for him. Dr Carmichael says: 'A belief prevails among Highlanders that every person is attended by an angel of light or by an angel of darkness . . . that during sleep the soul of the good accompanied by the angel of light ascends to the gates of heaven, there to foresee the bliss awaiting the good and brave; and that the soul of the bad accompanied by the bad angel descends to the gates of hell. . . . '

For many people today such conceptions may seem remote indeed. But they may be reminded of the psychological evidence that influences are at work in sleep and in dream which extend far beyond the reach of the ordinary waking mind; and that for the achievement of maturity and tranquillity, some kind of integration is necessary between the conscious self of waking life and the wider span of the Unconscious. The desire of the Highlander or Islander to prepare his mind, with the help of great words handed down to him, before he passes over into sleep, will seem, when we begin to take such things into account, as of great practical value. Students of Rudolf Steiner's work will recognise much here, once more, that is in harmony with his results.

Often in the same context as the archangels, great human beings are mentioned as well; the Apostles, and very often Columba and Bride. The fatherly protection of Columba was felt as something so near and essential for the Gaelic-speaking people that his festival was not celebrated simply once a year, but the Thursday in every week was felt as his day, and as propitious for all good work. (The remarks in 'The Auspicious Day' about the days of the week are of course not to be taken literally; the mother who does not want her son to leave home is weaving for him a tangle of difficulties. This poem may not seem either a prayer or a blessing; but it was regarded as having been very effective. The son stayed at home for the rest of his life.) The days of the week were felt strongly as having their individual character and needs; for example, no work necessitating the use of iron should be done on a Friday because of the nails of the Cross of Christ.

The attitude shown towards Columba in these poems is quite in accord with the picture given in his biography by St Adamnan, who was (in his own characteristic way) both a good historian and an artist. He describes how Columba's mother dreamed before his birth that she was given a beautiful cloak; but the cloak was then lifted into the sky and spread out over land and sea. Columba was in earthly fact a man concerned about everybody's troubles and hopes, both in the Ireland he had left, and among the people of Scotland to whom he had come. And we can understand that his concern is felt through the centuries as an abiding one; in these poems his cloak is still stretched out over land and sea. With Bride, or Brigit, we have something more mysterious; figures of different times have become one. But she is above all the beautiful, sisterly aid-woman of Mary; through her is expressed the Celtic sense of participation in the mystery of the Birth of Jesus.

The beings of the invisible worlds, whether angelic or human, are not thought to be concerned only with the well-being of man's soul – but also with his work, his crops and his animals. Cow or hen are not more or less efficient machinery for producing food, but have their own rights, and need of blessing. Through everything a harmonious order can and should work, if men are sufficiently awake to the helping power of the invisible.

This order is in the end the revelation of the Being of Christ. Without Him, nature has been in chaos, and would fall again into darkness. In the mysterious verses here called 'He Who was Crucified', in which it may be that fragments of several poems have been joined, we find this most uncompromisingly expressed:

> A time ere came the Son of God,
> The earth was a black morass,
> Without star, without sun, without moon,
> Without body, without heart, without form.
>
> Illumined plains, illumined hills,
> Illumined the great green sea,
> Illumined the whole globe together,
> When the Son of God came to earth.

If we believe that what the physicist can describe is the whole reality of sun or moon, such words may seem nonsense to us. But the measurements of a colour or of a sound – or of a human being – convey their reality only to a very limited extent. When the writers of these poems see the Christ through the light of the sun, or the growing field, or the breaking wave, they are restoring the unity of vision which the analysing mind could not help losing.

*　　*　　*

Each poem printed here is given complete, as in the

Carmina Gadelica – except that alternative readings have been omitted and choruses which are repeated are sometimes only indicated. At the end, the volume and page in the *Carmina* are given for each poem, and also, where this is stated, the name and home of the person from whom Dr Carmichael took down the original Gaelic. Hardly any notes have been added: once they began there seemed to be no telling where they would stop. A few examples have been given of Dr Carmichael's comments in his own words; the rest are condensations of explanations given by him. On the whole, it will be less important to know about points of detail in these poems, than to feel and to understand the kind of consciousness out of which they were born.

ADAM BITTLESTON

Morning and Evening

BLESSING OF THE KINDLING

I will kindle my fire this morning
In presence of the holy angels of heaven,
In presence of Ariel of the loveliest form,
In presence of Uriel of the myriad charms,
Without malice, without jealousy, without envy,
Without fear, without terror of any one under the sun,
But the Holy Son of God to shield me.
  Without malice, without jealousy, without envy,
  Without fear, without terror of any one under the
    sun,
  But the Holy Son of God to shield me.

God, kindle Thou in my heart within
A flame of love to my neighbour,
To my foe, to my friend, to my kindred all,
To the brave, to the knave, to the thrall,
O Son of the loveliest Mary,
From the lowliest thing that liveth,
To the Name that is highest of all.

THANKSGIVING

Thanks to Thee, O God, that I have risen today,
  To the rising of this life itself;
May it be to Thine own glory, O God of every gift,
  And to the glory of my soul likewise.

O great God, aid Thou my soul
  With the aiding of Thine own mercy;
Even as I clothe my body with wool,
  Cover Thou my soul with the shadow of Thy wing.

Help me to avoid every sin,
  And the source of every sin to forsake;
And as the mist scatters on the crest of the hills,
  May each ill haze clear from my soul, O God.

MORNING PRAYER

I believe, O God of all gods,
   That Thou art the eternal Father of life;
I believe, O God of all gods,
   That Thou art the eternal Father of love.

I believe, O God of all gods,
   That Thou art the eternal Father of the saints;
I believe, O God of all gods,
   That Thou art the eternal Father of each one.

I believe, O God of all gods,
   That Thou art the eternal Father of mankind;
I believe, O God of all gods,
   That Thou art the eternal Father of the world.

I believe, O Lord and God of the peoples,
That Thou art the creator of the high heavens,
That Thou art the creator of the skies above,
That Thou art the creator of the oceans below.

I believe, O Lord and God of the peoples,
   That Thou art He Who created my soul and set
     its warp,
Who created my body from dust and from ashes,
   Who gave to my body breath, and to my soul its
     possession.

       Father, bless to me my body,
       Father, bless to me my soul,
       Father, bless to me my life,
       Father, bless to me my belief.

Father eternal and Lord of the peoples,
  I believe that Thou hast remedied my soul in the
    Spirit of healing,
That Thou gavest Thy loved Son in covenant for me,
That Thou hast purchased my soul with the precious
    blood of Thy Son.

Father eternal and Lord of life,
  I believe that Thou didst pour on me the Spirit of
    grace at the bestowal of baptism

*   *   *
*   *   *

Father eternal and Lord of mankind,
Enwrap Thou my body and my soul beloved,
Safeguard me this night in the sanctuary of Thy
    love,
Shelter me this night in the shelter of the saints.

  Thou hast brought me up from last night
  To the gracious light of this day,
  Great joy to provide for my soul,
  And to do excelling good to me.

Thanks be to Thee, Jesu Christ,
  For the many gifts Thou hast bestowed on me,
Each day and night, each sea and land,
  Each weather fair, each calm, each wild.

I am giving Thee worship with my whole life,
  I am giving Thee assent with my whole power,
I am giving Thee praise with my whole tongue,
  I am giving Thee honour with my whole utterance.

6

I am giving Thee reverence with my whole under-
    standing,
  I am giving Thee offering with my whole thought,
I am giving Thee praise with my whole fervour,
  I am giving Thee humility in the blood of the Lamb.

I am giving Thee love with my whole devotion,
  I am giving Thee kneeling with my whole desire,
I am giving Thee love with my whole heart,
  I am giving Thee affection with my whole sense;
I am giving Thee my existence with my whole mind,
  I am giving Thee my soul, O God of all gods.

        My thought, my deed,
          My word, my will,
        My understanding, my intellect,
          My way, my state.

        I am beseeching Thee
        To keep me from ill,
        To keep me from hurt,
        To keep me from harm;
        To keep me from mischance,
        To keep me from grief,
        To keep me this night
          In the nearness of Thy love.

        May God shield me,
        May God fill me,
        May God keep me,
        May God watch me.

May God bring me
   To the land of peace,
   To the country of the King,
      To the peace of eternity.

Praise to the Father,
Praise to the Son,
Praise to the Spirit,
   The Three in One.

THE GUIDING LIGHT OF ETERNITY

O God, who broughtst me from the rest of last night
Unto the joyous light of this day,
Be Thou bringing me from the new light of this day
Unto the guiding light of eternity.
    Oh! from the new light of this day
    Unto the guiding light of eternity.

THE SLEEP PRAYER

I am now going into the sleep,
Be it that I in health shall waken;
If death be to me in the death-sleep,
Be it that on Thine own arm,
O God of Grace, I in peace shall waken;
  Be it on Thine own beloved arm,
    O God of Grace, that I in peace shall waken.

Be my soul on Thy right hand, O God,
Thou King of the heaven of heavens;
Thou it was who bought'st me with Thy blood,
Thou it was who gavest Thy life for me,
  Encompass Thou me this night, O God,
    That no harm, no evil shall me befall.

Whilst the body is dwelling in the sleep,
The soul is soaring in the shadow of heaven,
Be the red-white Michael meeting the soul,
Early and late, night and day,
  Early and late, night and day.

Amen.

THE GUARDIAN ANGEL

Thou angel of God who hast charge of me
From the dear Father of mercifulness,
The shepherding kind of the fold of the saints
To make round about me this night;

Drive from me every temptation and danger,
Surround me on the sea of unrighteousness,
And in the narrows, crooks, and straits,
Keep thou my coracle, keep it always.

Be thou a bright flame before me,
Be thou a guiding star above me,
Be thou a smooth path below me,
And be a kindly shepherd behind me,
Today, tonight, and for ever.

I am tired and I a stranger,
Lead thou me to the land of angels;
For me it is time to go home
To the court of Christ, to the peace of heaven.

SLEEP PRAYER

O Jesu without sin,
King of the poor,
Who wert sorely subdued
Under ban of the wicked,
Shield Thou me this night
From Judas.

My soul on Thine own arm, O Christ,
Thou the King of the City of Heaven,
Thou it was who bought'st my soul, O Jesu,
Thou it was who didst sacrifice Thy life for me.

Protect Thou me because of my sorrow,
For the sake of Thy passion, Thy wounds, and Thine
own blood,
And take me in safety tonight
Near to the City of God.

REPOSE

Thou Being of marvels,
Shield me with might,
Thou Being of statutes
    And of stars.

Compass me this night,
Both soul and body,
Compass me this night
    And on every night.

Compass me aright
Between earth and sky,
Between the mystery of Thy laws
    And mine eye of blindness;

Both that which mine eye sees
    And that which it reads not;
Both that which is clear
    And is not clear to my devotion.

I will smoor the hearth
As Mary would smoor;
The encompassment of Bride and of Mary,
On the fire and on the floor,
    And on the household all.

Who is on the lawn without?
Fairest Mary and her Son,
The mouth of God ordained, the angel of God spoke;
Angels of promise watching the hearth,
    Till white day comes to the fire.

The little drop of the Father
  On thy little forehead, beloved one.

The little drop of the Son
  On thy little forehead, beloved one.

The little drop of the Spirit
  On thy little forehead, beloved one.

To aid thee from the fays,
  To guard thee from the host;

To aid thee from the gnome,
  To shield thee from the spectre;

To keep thee for the Three,
  To shield thee, to surround thee;

To save thee for the Three,
  To fill thee with the graces;

The little drop of the Three
  To lave thee with the graces.

A wavelet for thy form,
A wavelet for thy voice,
  A wavelet for thy sweet speech;

A wavelet for thy luck,
A wavelet for thy good,
  A wavelet for thy health;

A wavelet for thy throat,
A wavelet for thy pluck,
  A wavelet for thy graciousness;
  Nine waves for thy graciousness.

THE BAPTISM BLESSING

Thou Being who inhabitest the heights
Imprint Thy blessing betimes,
Remember Thou the child of my body,
In Name of the Father of peace;
When the priest of the King
On him puts the water of meaning,
Grant him the blessing of the Three
    Who fill the heights.
  The blessing of the Three
    Who fill the heights.

Sprinkle down upon him Thy grace,
Give Thou to him virtue and growth,
Give Thou to him strength and guidance,
Give Thou to him flocks and possessions,
Sense and reason void of guile,
Angel wisdom in his day,
That he may stand without reproach
    In Thy presence.
  He may stand without reproach
    In Thy presence.

BATHING PRAYER

A palmful for thine age,
  A palmful for thy growth,
A palmful for thy throat,
  A flood for thine appetite.

For thy share of the dainty,
    Crowdie and kail;
For thy share of the taking,
  Honey and warm milk.

For thy share of the supping,
  Whisked whey and milk-product;
For thy share of the spoil,
  With bow and with spear.

For thy share of the preparation,
  The yellow eggs of Easter;
For thy share of the treat,
  My treasure and my joy,

For thy share of the feast
  With gifts and with tribute;
For thy share of the treasure,
  Pulset of my love.

For thy share of the chase
  Up the face of the Beinn-a-cheo;
For thy share of the hunting
  And the ruling over hosts.

For thy share of palaces,
   In the courts of kings;
For thy share of Paradise
   With its goodness and its peace.

The part of thee that does not grow at dawn,
   May it grow at eventide;
The part of thee that does not grow at night,
   May it grow at ridge of middle-day.

    The three palmfuls
    Of the Secret Three,
    To preserve thee
    From every envy,
    Evil eye and death;
    The palmful of the God of Life,
    The palmful of the Christ of Love,
    The palmful of the Spirit of Peace,
       Triune
       Of Grace.

THE INVOCATION OF THE GRACES

I bathe thy palms
In showers of wine,
In the lustral fire,
In the seven elements,
In the juice of the rasps,
In the milk of honey,
And I place the nine pure choice graces
In thy fair fond face,
 The grace of form,
 The grace of voice,
 The grace of fortune,
 The grace of goodness,
 The grace of wisdom,
 The grace of charity,
 The grace of choice maidenliness,
 The grace of whole-souled loveliness,
 The grace of goodly speech.

Dark is yonder town,
Dark are those therein,
Thou art the brown swan,
Going in among them.
Their hearts are under thy control,
Their tongues are beneath thy sole,
Nor will they ever utter a word
 To give thee offence.

A shade art thou in the heat,
A shelter art thou in the cold,
Eyes art thou to the blind,
A staff art thou to the pilgrim,

An island art thou at sea,
A fortress art thou on land,
A well art thou in the desert,
    Health art thou to the ailing.

Thine is the skill of the Fairy Woman,
Thine is the virtue of Bride the calm,
Thine is the faith of Mary the mild,
Thine is the tact of the woman of Greece,
Thine is the beauty of Emir the lovely,
Thine is the tenderness of Darthula delightful,
Thine is the courage of Maebh the strong,
    Thine is the charm of Binne-bheul.

Thou art the joy of all joyous things,
Thou art the light of the beam of the sun,
Thou art the door of the chief of hospitality,
Thou art the surpassing star of guidance,
Thou art the step of the deer of the hill,
Thou art the step of the steed of the plain,
Thou art the grace of the swan of swimming,
    Thou art the loveliness of all lovely desires.

The lovely likeness of the Lord
Is in thy pure face,
The loveliest likeness that
Was upon earth.

The best hour of the day be thine,
The best day of the week be thine,
The best week of the year be thine,
The best year in the Son of God's domain be thine.

Peter has come and Paul has come,
James has come and John has come,
Muriel and Mary Virgin have come,
Uriel the all-beneficent has come,
Ariel the beauteousness of the young has come,
Gabriel the seer of the Virgin has come,
Raphael the prince of the valiant has come,
And Michael the chief of the hosts has come,
    And Jesus Christ the mild has come,
    And the Spirit of true guidance has come,
    And the King of kings has come on the helm,
    To bestow on thee their affection and their love,
        To bestow on thee their affection and their
        love.

CHARM FOR THE FACE OF A MAIDEN

The beauty of God is in thy face,
The Son of God is protecting thee
From the wicked ones of the world,
The King of the stars is before thee.

The beauty of Mary of the deep love,
A tongue mannerly, mild, modest,
Fair hair between thy two eyebrows –
Fionn son of Cumhall between these.

Since it is Mary and Jesus her Son
Who set this pleasantness in thy face,
May the taste of mild honey be upon thee
And upon every word thou speakest,

To simple and to noble,
    To men and to tender women,
From this day that we have here
    Till the day of the ending of thy life.
In reliance on the beloved and the powers eternal,
In reliance on the God of life and the shielding of
    His Son.

MOTHER'S CONSECRATION

Be the great God between thy two shoulders
To protect thee in thy going and in thy coming,
Be the Son of Mary Virgin near thine heart,
And be the perfect Spirit upon thee pouring –
Oh, the perfect Spirit upon thee pouring!

THE AUSPICIOUS DAY

Thou man who wouldst travel tomorrow,
 Illinn ho ro hu o hu o
Tarry a little as thou art,
 Hillirinn ho ro hu o hu o
 Hillinn o i hu o ho i
 Ho hiura bhi hu o hu o
 Hill o a bha hillinn o ro
Till I make a shirt of thread for thee;
There is waiting and waiting for that:
The lint was sown but has not grown,
The wool is on the sheep of the wasteland,
The loom is in the wood of Patrick,
The beam is in the highest tree,
The shuttle is with the King of Spain,
The bobbin is with the Queen,
The weaver is not born to her mother,
Thou man who wouldst travel tomorrow,
Thou shalt not go on Monday nor shalt thou go on
 Tuesday,
Wednesday is tormenting, hurtful,
On Thursday are temptation and turbulence,
Friday is a day of rest,
Saturday is to the Mary Mother,
Let the Lord's Day praise the High King.
Thou man who wouldst travel strongly,
Thou shalt not go on Monday, the end of the quarter.

Thou man who wouldst travel lightly,
There is red blood upon thy shirt;
Not blood of roe nor blood of deer,
But blood of thy body and thou full of wounds.

GOOD WISH

Power of raven be thine,
Power of eagle be thine,
   Power of the Fiann.

Power of storm be thine,
Power of moon be thine,
   Power of sun.

Power of sea be thine,
Power of land be thine,
   Power of heaven.

    *   *   *

Goodness of sea be thine,
Goodness of earth be thine,
   Goodness of heaven.

Each day be joyous to thee,
No day be grievous to thee,
   Honour and compassion.

Love of each face be thine,
Death on pillow be thine,
   Thy Saviour's presence.

Give Thou to me, O God,
  Each food that is needful for my body;
Give Thou to me, O God,
Each light that is needful for my mind;
Give Thou to me, O God
  Each salve that is needful for my soul.

Give Thou to me, O God,
  Sincere repentance;
Give Thou to me, O God,
  Whole-hearted repentance;
Give Thou to me, O God,
  Lasting repentance.

Give Thou to me, O God,
  The death of the priceless oil;
Give Thou to me, O God,
  That the Healer of my soul be near me;
Give Thou to me, O God,
  The death of joy and of peace.

Give Thou to me, O God,
  To confess the death of Christ;
Give Thou to me, O God,
  To meditate the agony of Christ;
Give Thou to me, O God,
  To make warm the love of Christ.

O great God of Heaven,
  Draw Thou my soul to Thyself,
That I may make repentance
  With a right and a strong heart,

With a heart broken and contrite,
    That shall not change nor bend nor yield.

O great God of the angels,
    Bring Thou me to the dwelling of peace;
O great God of the angels,
    Preserve me from the evil of the fairies;
O great God of the angels,
    Bathe me in the bathing of Thy pool.

O great God of grace,
    Give Thou to me the strong Spirit of powers;
O great God of grace,
    Give Thou to me the Spirit undying, everlasting,
O great God of grace,
    Give Thou to me the loving Spirit of the Lamb.

THE DEATH BLESSING

God, omit not this man from Thy covenant,
And the many evils which he in the body committed,
That he cannot this night enumerate.
  The many evils that he in the body committed,
  That he cannot this night enumerate.

Be this soul on Thine own arm, O Christ,
Thou King of the City of Heaven,
And since Thine it was, O Christ, to buy the soul,
At the time of the balancing of the beam,
At the time of the bringing in the judgment,
Be it now on Thine own right hand,
  Oh! on Thine own right hand.

And be the holy Michael, king of angels,
Coming to meet the soul,
And leading it home
To the heaven of the Son of God.
  The Holy Michael, high king of angels,
  Coming to meet the soul,
  And leading it home
  To the heaven of the Son of God.

I AM GOING HOME WITH THEE

I am going home with thee
　To thy home! to thy home!
I am going home with thee
　To thy home of winter.

I am going home with thee
　To thy home! to thy home!
I am going home with thee
　To thy home of autumn,
　　of spring and of summer.

I am going home with thee,
　Thou child of my love,
To thine eternal bed
　To thy perpetual sleep.

I am going home with thee,
　Thou child of my love,
To the dear Son of blessings,
　To the Father of grace.

Work

THE CONSECRATION OF THE SEED

I will go out to sow the seed,
In name of Him who gave it growth;
I will place my front in the wind,
And throw a gracious handful on high.
Should a grain fall on a bare rock,
It shall have no soil in which to grow;
As much as falls into the earth
The dew will make it to be full.

Friday, day auspicious,
The dew will come down to welcome
Every seed that lay in sleep
Since the coming of cold without mercy;
Every seed will take root in the earth,
As the King of the elements desired,
The braird will come forth with the dew,
It will inhale life from the soft wind.

I will come round with my step,
I will go rightways with the sun,
In name of Ariel and the angels nine,
In name of Gabriel and the Apostles kind.
Father, Son, and Spirit Holy,
Be giving growth and kindly substance
To every thing that is in my ground,
Till the day of gladness shall come.

The Feast day of Michael, day beneficent,
I will put my sickle round about
The root of my corn as was wont;
I will lift the first cut quickly;

I will put it three turns round
My head, saying my rune the while,
My back to the airt of the north;
My face to the fair sun of power.

I shall throw the handful far from me,
I shall close my two eyes twice,
Should it fall in one bunch
My stacks will be productive and lasting;
No Carlin will come with bad times
To ask a palm bannock from us,
What time rough storms come with frowns
Nor stint nor hardship shall be on us.

REAPING BLESSING

God, bless Thou Thyself my reaping,
Each ridge, and plain, and field,
Each sickle curved, shapely, hard,
Each ear and handful in the sheaf,
    Each ear and handful in the sheaf.

Bless each maiden and youth,
Each woman and tender youngling,
Safeguard them beneath Thy shield of strength,
And guard them in the house of the saints,
    Guard them in the house of the saints.

Encompass each goat, sheep and lamb,
Each cow and horse, and store,
Surround Thou the flocks and herds,
And tend them to a kindly fold,
    Tend them to a kindly fold.

For the sake of Michael head of hosts,
Of Mary fair-skinned branch of grace,
Of Bride smooth-white of ringleted locks,
Of Columba of the graves and tombs,
    Columba of the graves and tombs.

MILKING BLESSING

Columba will give to her progeny,
Coivi the propitious, will give to her grass,
My speckled heifer will give me her milk,
And her female calf before her.
　　Ho my heifer! heifer! heifer!
　　Ho my heifer! kindly, calm,
　　My heifer gentle, gentle, beloved,
　　　　Thou art the love of thy mother.

Seest yonder thriving bramble bush
And the other bush glossy with brambles,
Such like is my fox-coloured heifer,
And her female calf before her.
　　　　Ho my heifer! –

The calm Bride of the white combs
Will give to my loved heifer the lustre of the swan,
While the loving Mary, of the combs of honey,
Will give to her the mottle of the heather hen.
　　　　Ho my heifer! –

MILKING SONGS

Bless, O God, my little cow,
  Bless, O God, my desire;
Bless Thou my partnership
  And the milking of my hands, O God

Bless, O God, each teat,
  Bless, O God, each finger;
Bless Thou each drop
  That goes into my pitcher, O God!

*   *   *

Give the milk, my treasure!
Give the milk, my treasure!
Give the milk, my treasure!

  Give the milk
  And thou'lt get a reward, –
  Bannock of quern,
  Sap of ale-wort,
  Wine of chalice,
  Honey and the wealth of the milk,
    My treasure!

  Give the milk
  And thou'lt get a reward, –
  Grasses of the plain,
  Milk of the fields,
  Ale of the malt,
  Music of the lyre,
    My treasure!

Give the milk, my treasure!
Give the milk my treasure!

Give the milk
And thou'lt have the blessing
Of the King of the earth,
The King of the sea,
The King of heaven,
The King of the angels,
The King of the City,
    My treasure!

*   *   *

Give the milk, my treasure,
Give quietly, with steady flow,
Give the milk, my treasure,
    With steady flow and calmly.

THE CLIPPING BLESSING

Go shorn and come woolly,
Bear the Beltane female lamb,
Be the lovely Bride thee endowing,
And the fair Mary thee sustaining,
    The fair Mary sustaining thee.

Michael the chief be shielding thee
From the evil dog and from the fox,
From the wolf and from the sly bear,
And from the taloned birds of destructive bills,
    From the taloned birds of hooked bills.

LOOM BLESSING

Thrums nor odds of thread
My hand never kept, nor shall keep,

Every colour in the bow of the shower
Has gone through my fingers beneath the cross,

White and black, red and madder,
Green, dark grey, and scarlet,

Blue, and roan, and colour of the sheep,
And never a particle of cloth was wanting.

I beseech calm Bride the generous,
I beseech mild Mary the loving,
I beseech Christ Jesu the humane,
That I may not die without them,
    That I may not die without them.

HATCHING BLESSING

I will rise early on the morning of Monday,
I will sing my rune and rhyme,
I will go sunwise with my cog
To the nest of my hen with sure intent.

I will place my left hand to my breast,
My right hand to my heart,
I will seek the loving wisdom of Him
Abundant in grace, in broods, and in flocks.

I will close my two eyes quickly,
As in blind-man's buff moving slowly;
I will stretch my left hand over thither
To the nest of my hen on yonder side.

The first egg which I shall bring near me,
I will put it withershins round my head.

*　　　*　　　*　　　*　　　*
*　　　*　　　*　　　*　　　*

I will raise my left hand on high,
I will stretch it without halt quickly,
I will lift the two eggs down hither,
There shall be then three in the cog.

I will stretch my right hand again,
I will lift with it at the time three,
I will seek ruling from the King,
Then verily there shall be six in the clutch.

I will raise my left hand the second time,
I will lift four with it down,
In name of Christ, King of power,
There shall then be ten in the cog.

The right fist of strongest claim,
I will lift with it two in my fingers,
Thus at ceasing my brood will be complete,
Beneath the breast of the speckled big hen.

I will put soot on their two ends,
And I dumb as the dumb the while,
In name of Creator of sea and hill,
In name of saints and apostles all.

In name of the most Holy Trinity,
In name of Columba kindly,
I will set the eggs on Thursday,
The gladsome brood will come on Friday.

SEA PRAYER

Helmsman: Blest be the boat.
Crew: God the Father bless her.
Helmsman: Blest be the boat.
Crew: God the Son bless her.
Helmsman: Blest be the boat.
Crew: God the Spirit bless her.
All: God the Father.
God the Son,
God the Spirit,
    Bless the boat.
Helmsman: What can befall you
And God the Father with you?
Crew: No harm can befall us.
Helmsman: What can befall you
And God the Son with you?
Crew: No harm can befall us.
Helmsman: What can befall you
And God the Spirit with you?
Crew: No harm can befall us.
All: God the Father,
God the Son,
God the Spirit,
    With us eternally.
Helmsman: What can cause you anxiety
And the God of the elements over you?
Crew: No anxiety can be ours.
Helmsman: What can cause you anxiety
And the King of the elements over you?
Crew: No anxiety can be ours.
Helmsman: What can cause you anxiety
And the Spirit of the elements over you?

45

Crew: No anxiety can be ours.
All: The God of the elements,
The King of the elements,
The Spirit of the elements,
Close over us,
Ever eternally.

The House

BLESSING OF THE HOUSE

May God give blessing
  To the house that is here;

May Jesus give blessing
  To the house that is here;

May Spirit give blessing
  To the house that is here;

May Three give blessing
  To the house that is here;

May Brigit give blessing
  To the house that is here;

May Michael give blessing
  To the house that is here;

May Mary give blessing
  To the house that is here;

May Columba give blessing
  To the house that is here;

Both crest and frame,
  Both stone and beam;

Both clay and wattle,
  Both summit and foundation;

Both window and timber,
  Both foot and head;

Both man and woman,
    Both wife and children;

Both young and old,
    Both maiden and youth;

    Plenty of food,
    Plenty of drink,
    Plenty of beds,
        Plenty of ale;

    Much of riches,
    Much of mirth,
    Many of people,
    Much of long life
        Be ever there:

Both warrior and poet,
    Both clay and beam;

Both gear and thong,
    Both crook and tie;

Both bairn and begetter,
    Both wife and children;

Both young and mature,
    Both maiden and youth.

May the King of the elements
    Be its help,
    The King of glory
        Have charge of it;

Christ the beloved,
     Son of Mary Virgin,
     And the gentle Spirit
          Be pouring therein;

Michael, bright warrior,
     King of the angels,
     Watch and ward it
          With the power of his sword;

And Brigit, the fair and tender,
     Her hue like the cotton-grass,
     Rich-tressed maiden
          Of ringlets of gold;

Mary, the fair and tender,
     Be nigh the hearth,
     And Columba kindly
     Giving benediction
     In fulfilment of each promise
          On those within,
          On those within!

GRACE BEFORE FOOD

Be with me, O God, at breaking of bread,
  Be with me, O God, at the close of my meal;
Let no whit adown my body
  That may hurt my sorrowing soul.
    O no whit adown my body
      That may hurt my sorrowing soul.

PEACE

The peace of God, the peace of men,
The peace of Columba kindly,
The peace of Mary mild, the loving,
The peace of Christ, King of tenderness,
  The peace of Christ, King of tenderness.

Be upon each window, upon each door,
Upon each hole that lets in light,
Upon the four corners of my house,
Upon the four corners of my bed,
  Upon the four corners of my bed;

Upon each thing my eye takes in,
Upon each thing my mouth takes in,
Upon my body that is of earth
And upon my soul that came from on high,
  Upon my body that is of earth
  And upon my soul that came from on high.

PEACE

Peace between neighbours,
Peace between kindred,
Peace between lovers,
    In love of the King of life.

Peace between person and person,
Peace between wife and husband,
Peace between woman and children,
The peace of Christ above all peace.

Bless, O Christ, my face,
    Let my face bless every thing;
Bless, O Christ, mine eye,
    Let mine eye bless all it sees.

Wonders of the World

JOURNEY BLESSING

Bless to me, O God,
  The earth beneath my foot,
Bless to me, O God,
  The path whereon I go;
Bless to me, O God,
  The thing of my desire;
    Thou Evermore of evermore,
  Bless Thou to me my rest.

Bless to me the thing
  Whereon is set my mind,
Bless to me the thing
  Whereon is set my love;
Bless to me the thing
  Whereon is set my hope;
    O Thou King of kings
  Bless Thou to me mine eye!

SUN

The eye of the great God,
The eye of the God of glory,
The eye of the King of hosts,
The eye of the King of the living
    Pouring upon us
      At each time and season,
    Pouring upon us
      Gently and generously.

    Glory to thee,
      Thou glorious sun.

Glory to thee, thou sun,
    Face of the God of life.

THE NEW MOON

She of my love is the new moon,
  The King of all creatures blessing her;
Be mine a good purpose
  Towards each creature of creation.

Holy be each thing
  Which she illumines;
Kindly be each deed
  Which she reveals.

Be her guidance on land
  With all beset ones;
Be her guidance on the sea
  With all distressed ones.

May the moon of moons
  Be coming through thick clouds
On me and on every mortal
  Who is coming through affliction.

May the virgin of my love
  Be coming through dense dark clouds
To me and to each one
  Who is in tribulation.

May the King of grace
  Be helping my hand
Now and for ever
  Till my resurrection day.

THE VOICE OF THUNDER

O God of the elements
O God of the mysteries
O God of the stars
   O King of kings!
   O King of kings!

Thy joy the joy,
Thy light the light,
Thy war the war,
   Thy peace the peace,
   Thy peace the peace.

Thy pain the pain,
Thy love the love,
That lasts for aye,
   To the end of ends,
   To the end of ends.

Thou pourest Thy grace
On those in distress,
On those in straits,
   Without stop or stint,
   Without stop or stint.

Thou Son of Mary of the Pasch,
Thou Son of Mary of the death,
Thou Son of Mary of the grace,
Who wast and shalt be
   With ebb and with flow;
Who wast and shalt be
   With ebb and with flow!

HE WHO WAS CRUCIFIED

Thou who wert hanged upon the tree,
   And wert crucified by the condemnation of the
      people,
Now that I am grown old and grey,
   Take to my confession-prayer, O God! pity.

No wonder to me great is my wickedness,
   I am a poor clattering cymbal,
In my youth I was profane,
   In my age I am forlorn.

A time ere came the Son of God,
   The earth was a black morass,
Without star, without sun, without moon,
   Without body, without heart, without form.

Illumined plains, illumined hills,
   Illumined the great green sea,
Illumined the whole globe together,
   When the Son of God came to earth.

Then it was that spoke the Mary of grace,
   The Virgin always most kindly and wise,
When Joseph gave to her his love,
   He desired to be often in her presence.

A compact there was between Joseph and Virgin,
   In order well-becoming and just,
That the compact might be confirmed
   By the seal of the Great King of virtues.

They went with him to the Temple of God,
   Where the clerics sat within:
As ordained of the Great High King,
   They married ere they came out.

An angel came afterwards: –
   'Joseph, why excited thou?'
'I got a woman from the clerics,
   It is not natural for me to be calm.'

'Joseph, abide thou by thy reason,
   Not enlightened of thee to find fault,
What thou hast gotten is a virgin pure,
   On whom man never put hand.'

'How can I believe that from thee?
   I myself, my grief! have knowledge –
When I laid me down by her shoulder
   A living child beneath her girdle throbbed.'

PEACE

The peace of joys,
The peace of lights,
The peace of consolations.

The peace of souls,
The peace of heaven,
The peace of the virgins.

The peace of the fairy bowers,
The peace of peacefulness,
The peace of everlasting.

Omens and Sorrows

OMENS

Early on the morning of a Monday,
I heard the bleating of a lamb.

And the kid-like cry of snipe,
While gently sitting bent,

And the grey-blue cuckoo,
And no food on my stomach.

On the fair evening of Tuesday,
I saw on the smooth stone,
The snail slimy, pale.

And the ashy wheatear,
On the top of the dyke of holes,

The foal of the old mare,
Of spranchly gait and its back to me.

And I knew from these,
That the year would not rise with me.

POEM OF THE FLOOD

On Monday will come the great storm
Which the airy firmament will pour,
We shall be obedient the while,
   All who will hearken.

On Tuesday will come the other element,
Heart paining, hard piercing,
Wringing from pure pale cheeks
   Blood, like showers of wine.

On Wednesday will blow the wind,
Sweeping bare strath and plain
Showering gusts of galling grief
   Thunder bursts and rending hills.

On Thursday will pour the shower,
Driving people into blind flight,
Faster than the foliage on the trees,
   Like the leaves of Mary's plant in terror trembling.

On Friday will come the dool cloud of darkness
The direst dread that ever came over the world,
Leaving multitudes bereft of reason,
   Grass and fish beneath the same flagstone.

On Saturday will come the great sea,
Rushing like a mighty river;
All will be at their best
   Hastening to a hill of safety.

On Sunday will arise my King,
Full of ire and tribulation,
Listening to the bitter talk of each man,
  A red cross on each right shoulder.

THE LULLABY OF THE SNOW

Cold, cold this night is my bed,
Cold, cold this night is my child,
Lasting, lasting this night thy sleep,
I in my shroud and thou in mine arm.

Over me creeps the shadow of death,
The warm pulse of my love will not stir,
The wind of the heights thy sleep-lulling,
The close-clinging snow of the peaks thy mantle.

Over thee creeps the hue of death,
White angels are floating in the air,
The Son of grace each season guards thee,
The Son of my God keeps the watch with me.

Though loud my cry my plaint is idle,
Though sore my struggle no friend shares it;
Thy body-shirt is the snow of the peaks,
Thy death-bed the fen of the valleys.

Thine eye is closed, thy sleep is heavy,
Thy mouth to my breast, but thou seekest no milk;
My croon of love thou shalt never know,
My plaint of love thou shalt never tell.

A cold arm-burden my love on my bosom,
A frozen arm-burden without life or breath;
May the angels of God make smooth the road,
May the angels of God be calling us home.

A hard frost no thaw shall subdue,
The frost of the grave which no spring shall make
    green,
A lasting sleep which morn shall not break,
The death-slumber of mother and child.

Heavenly light directs my feet,
The music of the skies gives peace to my soul,
Alone I am under the wing of the Rock,
Angels of God calling me home.

Cold, cold, cold is my child,
Cold, cold is the mother who watches thee,
Sad, sad, sad is my plaint,
As the tinge of death creeps over me.

O Cross of the heavens, sign my soul,
O Mother of breastlings, shield my child,
O Son of tears whom a mother nurtured,
Show thy tenderness in death to the needy.

MELODIOUS ONE OF THE MOUNTAINS

My lover found me in my sleep,
  I wearying for his coming;
I crouching beneath rough rocks,
  Oh King! how shameful the condition.

I without understanding or reason,
  Oh King! tearful was the awaking;
That grace for which I seek
  'Tis a breath of the Spirit of prayer.

It was Thou, O King Who art on the throne,
  Who didst make for me the day in its season;
I in the wilderness of the mountains,
  Thy warmth sheltered me from the cold.

Many are the ways of evil habits
  To disturb the flesh of the sinful;
O Christ, ere I am laid in the tomb
  Place Thou the power of Thy righteousness within
    me.

Thou throned King of glory,
  Thou great Being Who hast redeemed me
From the foolish ways of sin
  To which my nature cleaves;

From the sins corrupt
  Which have caused temptation to my soul,
From the sins deceiving
  That would conquer me despite my will.

Though mine were the world
    And all the wealth upon its surface,
Though mine were every treasure,
    All pomp and all grandeur;

Though I should get and have them in my grasp,
    I would give them all away,
If but the Father of salvation
    Might with His arm encircle me.

O Thou great God enthroned,
    Succour me betimes with Thy goodness;
Make my sins unclean
    To part from me this night.

For the sake of Thine anguish and Thy tears,
    For the sake of Thy pain and Thy passion,
Good Son of Mary, be in peace with me
    And succour me at my death!

Thou art my precious Lord,
    Thou art my strong pillar,
Thou art the sustenance of my breast:
    Oh part Thou from me never!

For mine afflictions forsake me not,
    For my tears' sake do not leave me!
Jesu! Thou likeness of the sun,
    In the day of my need be near me!

Thou great Lord of the sun,
    In the day of my need be near me;
Thou great Being of the universe,
    Keep me in the surety of Thine arms!

Leave me not in dumbness,
  Dead in the wilderness;
Leave me not to my stumbling,
  For my trust is in Thee, my Saviour!

Though I had no fire,
  Thy warmth did not fail me;
Though I had no clothing,
  Thy love did not forsake me.

Though I had no hearth,
  The cold did not numb me;
Though I knew not the ways,
  Thy knowledge was around me.

Though I was in weakness,
  The hinds showed me kindness;
Though I had no light,
  The night was as the day.

Though I had no bed,
  I lacked not for sleep,
For Christ's arm was my pillow,
  His eye supreme was my protection.

Though I was forlorn,
  Hunger came not near me,
For Christ's Body was my food,
  The Blood of Christ, it was my drink.

Though I was without reason,
  Thou forsookest me not a moment;
Though I was without sense,
  Thou didst not choose to leave me.

Though the stones were diamonds,
   Though they were dollars of gold,
Though the whole ocean were wine,
   Offered to me of right;

Though the earth were of cinnamon
   And the lakes were of honey,
Dearer were a vision of Christ
   In peace, in love, in pity.

Jesu, meet Thou my soul!
   Jesu, clothe me in Thy love!
Jesu, shield Thou my spirit!
   Jesu, stretch out to me Thine hand!

AUGURY OF MARY

God over me, God under me,
God before me, God behind me,
I on Thy path, O God,
   Thou, O God, in my steps.

The augury made of Mary to her Son,
The offering made of Bride through her palm,
Sawest Thou it, King of life? –
   Said the King of life that He saw.

The augury made by Mary for her own offspring
When He was for a space amissing,
Knowledge of truth, not knowledge of falsehood,
   That I shall truly see all my quest.

Son of beauteous Mary, King of life,
Give Thou me eyes to see all my quest,
With grace that shall never fail, before me,
   That shall never quench nor dim.

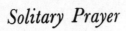

Solitary Prayer

RUNE BEFORE PRAYER

I am bending my knee
In the eye of the Father who created me,
In the eye of the Son who purchased me,
In the eye of the Spirit who cleansed me,
   In friendship and affection.
Through Thine own Anointed One, O God,
Bestow upon us fulness in our need,
     Love towards God,
     The affection of God,
     The smile of God,
     The wisdom of God,
     The grace of God,
     The fear of God,
     And the will of God
To do on the world of the Three,
As angels and saints
Do in heaven;
   Each shade and light,
   Each day and night,
   Each time in kindness,
   Give Thou us Thy Spirit.

PRAYER

O God, hearken to my prayer,
Let my earnest petition come to Thee
For I know that Thou art hearing me
As surely as though I saw Thee with mine eyes.

I am placing a lock upon my heart,
  I am placing a lock upon my thoughts,
I am placing a lock upon my lips
  And double-knitting them.

Aught that is amiss for my soul
  In the pulsing of my death,
Mayest Thou, O God, sweep it from me
  And mayest Thou shield me in the blood of Thy
    love.

Let no thought come to my heart,
Let no sound come to mine ear,
Let no temptation come to mine eye,
Let no fragrance come to my nose,

Let no fancy come to my mind,
Let no ruffle come to my spirit,
That is hurtful to my poor body this night,
Nor ill for my soul at the hour of my death;

But mayest Thou Thyself, O God of life,
Be at my breast, be at my back,
Thou to me as a star, Thou to me as a guide,
From my life's beginning to my life's closing.

PRAYER

Pray I this day my prayer to Thee, O God,
Voice I this day as voices the voice of thy mouth,
Keep I this day as keep the people of heaven,
Spend I this day as spend Thine own household,

Go I this day according to Thy laws, O God,
Pass I this day as pass the saints in heaven.

Thou loving Christ Who wast hanged upon the tree
Each day and each night remember I Thy covenant;
In my lying down and rising up I yield me to Thy
      cross,
In my life and my death my health Thou art and my
      peace.

Each day may I remember the source of the mercies
   Thou hast bestowed on me gently and generously;
Each day may I be fuller in love to Thyself
        *   *   *

Each thing I have received, from Thee it came,
Each thing for which I hope, from Thy love it will
      come,
Each thing I enjoy, it is of Thy bounty,
Each thing I ask, comes of Thy disposing.

Holy God, loving Father, of the word everlasting,
Grant me to have of Thee this living prayer;
Lighten my understanding, kindle my will, begin my
      doing,
Incite my love, strengthen my weakness, enfold my
      desire.

Cleanse my heart, make holy my soul, confirm my
        faith,
Keep safe my mind and compass my body about;
As I utter my prayer from my mouth
In mine own heart may I feel Thy presence.

And do Thou grant, O God of life,
That Thou be at my breast, that Thou be at my back,
That Thou give me my needs as may befit the crown
    Thou hast promised to us in the world beyond.

And grant Thou to me, Father beloved,
From Whom each thing that is freely flows,
That no tie over-strict, no tie over-dear
    May be between myself and this world below.

        Place I in Thee my hope, O God,
        My living hope in the Father of the heavens,
        My great hope to be with Thyself
            In the distant world to come.

        Father and Son and Spirit,
            The One Person of the Three,
        Perfect, world without end,
            Changeless through life eternal.

THOUGHTS

God's will would I do,
My own will bridle;

God's due would I give,
My own due yield;

God's path would I travel,
My own path refuse;

Christ's death would I ponder,
My own death remember;

Christ's agony would I meditate,
My love to God make warmer;

Christ's cross would I carry,
My own cross forget;

Repentance of sin would I make,
Early repentance choose;

A bridle to my tongue I would put,
A bridle on my thoughts I would keep;

God's judgment would I judge,
My own judgment guard;

Christ's redemption would I seize,
My own ransom work;

The love of Christ would I feel,
My own love know.

PRAYER TO JESUS

I say the prayer from my mouth,
I say the prayer from my heart,
I say the prayer to Thee Thyself,
  O Healing Hand, O Son of the God of salvation;

O Son of Mary the benign,
Together with Pater and Credo,
The Prayer of Mary thereafter,
  And Thine own Prayer, O Son of the God of grace;

To magnify the greatness of heaven
To magnify the greatness of God,
To magnify Thine own greatness,
  And Thy glory, O Son of God of the Passion;

To give praise to Thee, Jesus,
Lord of sea and of land,
Lord of sun and of moon,
  Lord of the beautiful stars.

Fountain of life to the righteous,
  Faithful Brother of helpfulness,
Make Thou my prayer availing
  To my soul and to my body.

Thou Lord God of the angels,
Spread over me Thy linen robe;
Shield me from every famine,
Free me from every spectral shape.

Strengthen me in every good,
Encompass me in every strait,
Safeguard me in every ill,
And from every venom restrain me.

Be Thou between me and all things grisly,
Be Thou between me and all things mean,
Be Thou between me and all things gruesome
  Coming darkly towards me.

O glorious Master of the clouds,
O glorious Master of the skies,
O glorious Master of the heavens,
  Blest by Thee has been every tribe and people.

  Intercede Thou for me
  With the Lord God of life,
  With the kind Father of glory,
    With the great Chief of the nations.

  O Master endeared,
  O Master bright, fragrant,
  O Master beloved,
  O Master bright, kindly,
  I beseech Thee with earnestness,
  I beseech Thee with humbleness,
  I beseech Thee with lowliness,
  I beseech Thee with tearfulness,
  I beseech Thee with kneeling,
    That Thou not forsake me
      In the passion of my death;

But that I might find rest everlasting
In the repose of the Trinity,
In the Paradise of the godly,
  In the Vine-garden of Thy love.

Put Thy salve to my sight,
Put Thy balm to my wounds,
Put Thy linen robe to my skin,
  O Healing Hand, O Son of the God of salvation.

    O God of the weak,
    O God of the lowly,
    O God of the righteous,
      O shield of homesteads:

    Thou art calling upon us
    In the voice of glory,
    With the mouth of mercy
      Of Thy beloved Son.

O may I find rest everlasting
In the home of Thy Trinity,
In the Paradise of the godly,
  In the Sun-garden of Thy love.

GOD WITH ME LYING DOWN

God with me lying down,
God with me rising up,
God with me in each ray of light,
Nor I a ray of joy without Him,
    Nor one ray without Him.

Christ with me sleeping,
Christ with me waking,
Christ with me watching,
Every day and night,
    Each day and night.

God with me protecting,
The Lord with me directing,
The Spirit with me strengthening,
For ever and for evermore,
    Ever and evermore, Amen.
        Chief of chiefs, Amen.

The Feasts of the Year

Hail King! hail King! blessed is He! blessed is He!
Hail King! hail King! blessed is He! blessed is He!
Hail King! hail King! blessed is He, the King of
       whom we sing,
    All hail! let there be joy!

This night is the eve of the great Nativity,
Born is the Son of Mary the Virgin,
The soles of His feet have reached the earth,
The Son of glory down from on high,
Heaven and earth glowed to Him,
    All hail! let there be joy!

The peace of earth to Him, the joy of heaven to Him,
Behold His feet have reached the world;
The homage of a King be His, the welcome of a
       Lamb be His,
King all victorious, Lamb all glorious,
Earth and ocean illumed to Him,
    All hail! let there be joy!

The mountains glowed to Him, the plains glowed to
       Him,
The voice of the waves with the song of the strand,
Announcing to us that Christ is born,
Son of the King of kings from the land of salvation;
Shone the sun on the mountains high to Him,
    All hail! let there be joy!

Shone to Him the earth and sphere together,
God the Lord has opened a Door;
Son of Mary Virgin, hasten Thou to help me,
Thou Christ of hope, Thou Door of joy,
Golden Sun of hill and mountain,
    All hail! let there be joy!

PRAISE OF MARY

I say the prayer
That was given with anointing
To the Mary Mother
    Of joy;

Along with Pater and Credo,
The Prayer of Mary besides,
And the Prayer of God's Son
    Of the Passion;

To magnify thine own honour,
To magnify the glory of God's Son,
To magnify the greatness of the God
    Of grace.

Plead with thy gracious Son
That He make my prayer avail
My soul, and thereafter
    My body.

Thou Queen of the angels,
Thou Queen of the kingdom,
Thou Queen of the city
    Of glory:

Enfold me in every virtue,
Encompass me from every vice
  *   *   *   *
      *   *

Thou shining Mother of gentleness,
Thou glorious Mother of the stars
Blessed hast thou been of every race
     And people.

O thou, alone praised, worthy of praise,
Make fervent prayer for me
With the Lord of the worlds,
     The God of life.

Thou Mary, gentle, fair, gracious,
I pray that thou forsake me not
In the sharp pang
     Of my death.

Shield of every dwelling, shield of every people,
That are sorely calling
On the gracious mercy
     Of thy dear Son:

Thou art the Queen-maiden of sweetness,
Thou art the Queen-maiden of faithfulness,
Thou art the Queen-maiden of peacefulness,
     And of the peoples.

Thou art the well of compassion,
Thou art the root of consolations,
Thou art the living stream of the virgins
     And of them who bear child.

Thou art the tabernacle of Christ,
Thou art the mansion of Christ,
Thou art the ark of Christ –
     Of Him alone.

Thou art the Queen-maiden of the sea,
Thou art the Queen-maiden of the kingdom,
Thou art the Queen-maiden of the angels,
    In effulgence.

Thou art the temple of the God of life,
Thou art the tabernacle of the God of life,
Thou art the mansion of the God of life
    And of the forlorn.

Thou art the river of grace,
Thou art the well-spring of salvation
Thou art the garden and the paradise
    Of the virgins.

Thou art the star of morning,
Thou art the star of watching,
Thou art the star of the ocean
    Great.

Thou art the star of the earth,
Thou art the star of the kingdom,
Thou art the star of the Son of the Father
    Of glory.

Thou art the corn of the land,
Thou art the treasury of the sea,
The wished-for visitant of the homes
    Of the world.

Thou art the vessel of fulness,
Thou art the cup of wisdom,
Thou art the well-spring of health
    Of mankind.

Thou art the garden of virtues,
Thou art the mansion of gladness,
Thou art the Mother of sadness
    And of clemency.

Thou art the garden of apples,
Thou art the lull-song of the great folks,
Thou art the fulfilment of the world's desire
    In loveliness.

Thou art the sun of the heavens,
Thou art the moon of the skies,
Thou art the star and the path
    Of the wanderers.

Since thou art the full ocean,
    Pilot me at sea;
Since thou art the dry shore,
    Save me upon land.

Since thou art the gem of the jewel,
Save me from fire and from water,
Save me from sky-hosts of evil
    And from fairy shafts.

There is none who utters my song
    Or puts it into use,
But Mary will show herself to him
    Three times before his death and his end.

THE VIRGIN

The Virgin was beheld approaching,
Christ so young on her breast,
Angels bowing lowly before them,
And the King of life was saying, 'Tis meet.

The Virgin of locks most glorious,
The Jesus more gleaming-white than snow,
Seraphs melodious singing their praise,
And the King of life was saying, 'Tis meet.

O Mary Mother of wondrous power,
Grant us the succour of thy strength,
Bless the provision, bless the board,
Bless the ear, the corn, the food.

The Virgin of mien most glorious,
The Jesus more gleaming-white than snow,
She like the moon in the hills arising,
He like the sun on the mountain-crests.

The people say that the sun dances on this day in joy for a risen Saviour.

Old Barbara Macphie at Dreimsdale saw this once, but only once, during her long life. And the good woman, of high natural intelligence, described in poetic language and with religious fervour what she saw or believed she saw from the summit of Benmore:

'The glorious gold-bright sun was after rising on the crests of the great hills, and it was changing colour – green, purple, red, blood-red, white, intense-white, and gold-white, like the glory of the God of the elements to the children of men. It was dancing up and down in exultation at the joyous resurrection of the beloved Saviour of victory.

'To be thus privileged, a person must ascend to the top of the highest hill before sunrise, and believe that the God who makes the small blade of grass to grow is the same God who makes the large, massive sun to move.'

THE BELTANE BLESSING

Bless, O Threefold true and bountiful,
Myself, my spouse, and my children,
My tender children and their beloved mother at their
    head.
On the fragrant plain, on the gay mountain sheiling,
  On the fragrant plain, on the gay mountain sheiling.

Everything within my dwelling or in my possession,
All kine and crops, all flocks and corn,
From Hallow Eve to Beltane Eve,
With goodly progress and gentle blessing,
From sea to sea, and every river mouth,
  From wave to wave, and base of waterfall.

Be the Three Persons taking possession of all to me
    belonging,
Be the sure Trinity protecting me in truth;
Oh! satisfy my soul in the words of Paul,
And shield my loved ones beneath the wing of Thy
    glory,
  Shield my loved ones beneath the wing of Thy
    glory.

Bless everything and every one,
Of this little household by my side;
Place the cross of Christ on us with the power of love,
Till we see the land of joy,
  Till we see the land of joy.

What time the kine shall forsake the stalls,
What time the sheep shall forsake the folds,

What time the goats shall ascend to the mount of
    mist,
May the tending of the Triune follow them,
  May the tending of the Triune follow them.

Thou being who didst create me at the beginning,
Listen and attend me as I bend the knee to Thee,
Morning and evening as is becoming in me,
In Thine own presence, O God of life,
  In Thine own presence, O God of life.

HYMN OF THE PROCESSION

Valiant Michael of the white steeds,
Who subdued the Dragon of blood,
For love of God, for pains of Mary's Son,
Spread thy wing over us, shield us all,
  Spread thy wing over us, shield us all.

Mary beloved! Mother of the White Lamb,
Shield, oh shield us, pure Virgin of nobleness,
And Bride, the beauteous, shepherdess of the flocks.
Safeguard thou our cattle, surround us together,
  Safeguard thou our cattle, surround us together.

And Columba, beneficent, benign,
In name of Father, and of Son, and of Spirit Holy,
Through the Three-in-One, through the Trinity,
Encompass thou ourselves, shield our procession,
  Encompass thou ourselves, shield our procession.

O Father! O Son! O Spirit Holy!
Be the Triune with us day and night,
On the machair plain or on the mountain ridge
Be the Triune with us and His arm around our head,
  Be the Triune with us and His arm around our head.

Barra Fishermen:

O Father! O Son! O Spirit Holy!
Be thou, Three-One, with us day and night,
And on the back of the wave as on the mountain side
Our Mother shall be with us with her arm under our
head.

    And on the back of the wave as on the mountain
side

    Our Mother shall be with us with her arm under
our head.

HOLY SPIRIT

O Holy Spirit of greatest power,
Come down upon us and subdue us;
From Thy glorious mansion in the heavens,
Thy light effulgent shed on us.

Father beloved of every naked one,
From Whom all gifts and goodness come,
Our hearts illumine with Thy mercy,
In Thy mercy shield us from all harm.

Without Thy divinity there is nothing
In man that can earn esteem;
Without Thyself, O King of kings,
Sinless man can never be.

In succour Thou art of all the best
Against the soul of wildest speech;
Food art thou sweeter than all;
Sustain and guide us at every time.

The knee that is stiff, O Healer, make pliant,
The heart that is hard make warm beneath Thy wing;
The soul that is wandering from Thy path,
Grasp Thou his helm and he shall not die.

Each thing that is foul cleanse Thou early,
Each thing that is hard soften Thou with Thy grace,
Each wound that is working us pain,
O Best of healers, make Thou whole!

Give Thou to Thy people to be diligent
To put their trust in Thee as God,
That Thou mayest help them in every hour
With thy sevenfold gift, O Holy Spirit generous!

THE FEAST DAY OF MARY

On the feast day of Mary the fragrant,
Mother of the Shepherd of the flocks,
I cut me a handful of the new corn,
I dried it gently in the sun,
I rubbed it sharply from the husk
    With mine own palms.

I ground it in a quern on Friday,
I baked it on a fan of sheep-skin,
I toasted it to a fire of rowan,
And I shared it round my people.

I went sunways round my dwelling,
In name of the Mary Mother,
Who promised to preserve me,
Who did preserve me,
And who will preserve me,
In peace, in flocks,
In righteousness of heart.

In labour, in love,
In wisdom, in mercy,
For the sake of Thy Passion.
Thou Christ of grace
Who till the day of my death
Wilt never forsake me!
    Oh, till the day of my death
    Wilt never forsake me!

MICHAEL THE VICTORIOUS

Thou Michael the victorious,
I make my circuit under thy shield,
Thou Michael of the white steed,
And of the bright brilliant blades,
Conqueror of the dragon,
Be thou at my back,
Thou ranger of the heavens,
Thou warrior of the King of all,
    O Michael the victorious,
    My pride and my guide,
    O Michael the victorious,
    The glory of mine eye.

I make my circuit
In the fellowship of my saint,
On the machair, on the meadow,
On the cold heathery hill;
Though I should travel ocean
And the hard globe of the world
No harm can e'er befall me
'Neath the shelter of thy shield;
    O Michael the victorious,
    Jewel of my heart,
    O Michael the victorious,
    God's shepherd thou art.

Be the sacred Three of Glory
Aye at peace with me,
With my horses, with my cattle,
With my woolly sheep in flocks.
With the crops growing in the field

Or ripening in the sheaf,
On the machair, on the moor,
In cole, in heap, or stack.
    Every thing on high or low,
    Every furnishing and flock,
    Belong to the holy Triune of glory,
    And to Michael the victorious.

MICHAEL MILITANT

O Michael Militant,
    Thou king of the angels,
Shield thy people
    With the power of thy sword,
        Shield thy people
        With the power of thy sword.

Spread thy wing
    Over sea and land,
East and west,
    And shield us from the foe,
        East and west,
        And shield us from the foe.

Brighten thy feast
    From heaven above;
Be with us in the pilgrimage
    And in the twistings of the fight;
        Be with us in the pilgrimage
        And in the twistings of the fight.

Thou chief of chiefs,
    Thou chief of the needy,
Be with us in the journey
    And in the gleam of the river;
        Be with us in the journey
        And in the gleam of the river.

Thou chief of chiefs,
    Thou chief of angels,
Spread thy wing
    Over sea and land,

For thine is their fullness,
Thine is their fullness,
    Thine own is their fullness,
    Thine own is their fullness.

Columba and Bride

THE DAY OF SAINT COLUMBA

Thursday of Columba benign,
Day to send sheep on prosperity,
Day to send cow on calf,
Day to put the web in the warp.

Day to put coracle on the brine,
Day to place the staff to the flag,
Day to bear, day to die,
Day to hunt the heights.

Day to put horses in harness,
Day to send herds to pasture,
Day to make prayer efficacious,
Day of my beloved, the Thursday,
    Day of my beloved, the Thursday.

COLUMBA'S HERDING

May the herding of Columba
Encompass you going and returning,
Encompass you in strath and on ridge
    And on the edge of each rough region;

May it keep you from pit and from mire,
Keep you from hill and from crag,
Keep you from loch and from downfall,
    Each evening and each darkling;

May it keep you from the mean destroyer,
Keep you from the mischievous niggard,
Keep you from the mishap of bar-stumbling
    And from the untoward fays.

The peace of Columba be yours in the grazing,
    The peace of Brigit be yours in the grazing,
The peace of Mary be yours in the grazing,
    And may you return home safe-guarded.

SAINT JOHN'S WORT

I will cull my plantlet,
As a prayer to my King,
To quiet the wrath of men of blood,
To check the wiles of wanton women.

I will cull my plantlet,
As a prayer to my King,
That mine may be its power
Over all I see.

I will cull my plantlet,
As a prayer to the Three,
Beneath the shade of the Triune of grace,
And of Mary the Mother of Jesu.

BRIDE THE AID-WOMAN

There came to me assistance,
Mary fair and Bride;
As Anna bore Mary,
As Mary bore Christ,
As Eile bore John the Baptist
Without flaw in him,
Aid thou me in mine unbearing,
    Aid me, O Bride!

As Christ was conceived of Mary
Full perfect on every hand,
Assist thou me, foster-mother,
The conception to bring from the bone;
And as thou didst aid the Virgin of joy,
Without gold, without corn, without kine,
Aid thou me, great is my sickness,
    Aid me, O Bride.

Conclusion

FRAGMENT

As it was,
As it is,
As it shall be
Evermore,
O Thou Triune
Of grace!
With the ebb
With the flow,
O Thou Triune
Of grace!
With the ebb
With the flow.

SOURCES

MORNING AND EVENING

AGES OF LIFE

19   (I. 61)   Taken down at Creagorry, Benbecula, on 16th December, 1872, from Janet Campbell, nurse, South Uist. *Beinn-a-cheo*, mount of mist: probably a particular name and not a general term (II.229).

21   (I. 7)   Duncan MacLellan, crofter, South Uist, heard this poem from Catherine Macaulay in the early years of this [the nineteenth] century. I heard versions of this poem in other islands and in districts of the mainland. The poem must have been widely known. In Tiree the poem was addressed to boys and girls, in Uist to young men and maidens. Probably it was composed to a maiden on her marriage. The phrase *eala dhonn*, brown swan, would indicate that the girl was young, not yet a white swan (I.6). The seven elements would probably be fire, air, earth, water, snow, ice and wind—perhaps lightning (II.349). *Binne-bheul*: mouth of melody, a character in Gaelic story. The people say that the birds of the air, the beasts of the field, and the fishes of the sea stood still and listened when Binne-bheul sang (II.231).

24   (III.227)   No source given. *Fionn* means fair.

25   (II.171)   From Mairiread MacLeod, crofter's wife, Benbecula. These lines are whispered by mothers into the ears of sons and daughters when leaving their homes in the Outer Isles for the towns of the south and for foreign lands (II.170).

26   (v.323)   From Christine Gillies, Benbecula. Also from Mary MacDonald, wife of Alexander MacNeill, Barra, September 1872.

27   (III.231)   From Mary Mackintosh, South Uist.

28   (III.389)   From Ann MacDonald, widow, from Lochaber.

30   (I.119)   From Donald MacDonald, crofter, South Uist.

31   (III.379)   Dr Carmichael obtained four or five versions
                 of this poem in Lewis.

WORK

35   (I.243)   From Lachlan MacDonald, crofter, Benbecula.
37   (I.247)   From Angus MacDonald, crofter, South Uist.
38   (I.263)   From Mairiread MacRae, crofter's wife, South
                Uist. Coivi: the traditional archdruid of the
                Celts (II.256). The cows become accus-
                tomed to these lilts, and will not give their
                milk without them, nor occasionally without
                their favourite airs being sung to them
                (I.258).
39   (IV. 65, 67)   No names are given.
41   (I.293)   From Malcolm MacPherson, shepherd, South
                Uist.
42   (I.301)   From Mary Wilson, weaver, Benbecula.
43   (I.285)   From Donald MacLean, farmer, native of
                Small Isles.
45   (I.333)   From Gilleaspuig MacLellan, shipmaster,
                South Uist.

THE HOUSE

49   (III.361)   From Alexander Maclean, Tiree.
52   (III.315)   From Malcolm Macmillan, merchant, Ben-
                 becula.
53   (III.265)   No name is given.
54   (III.267)   From Mary MacLeod, Gairloch.

WONDERS OF THE WORLD

57   (III.181)   Dugall MacAulay, cottar, Benbecula.
58   (III.307)   Fragments were obtained from a man of
                 ninety-nine years in the south end of South
                 Uist, and from another in Mingulay, Barra.
59, 60 (III.299, 271)   No names are given.
61   (II.173)   In Kintail, from Alexander Matheson, ship-
                 master, Lochalsh.
63   (III.269)   No name is given.

67   (ii.179)   From Ceit MacInnes, cottar, Arasaig.

68   (i.225)   From Roderick MacDonald, farmer, North Uist.

70   (iv.345)   From John Macnab, student of divinity, Glen Orchy, and Big Peter MacDonald of Glen Coe. The night after the massacre of Glen Coe, officers and soldiers were out searching the hills and dales for any stray fugitives who might have escaped the massacre (iv.345). One such soldier is said to have found a woman who was singing this song, nursing her child in the snow. Moved to pity, he disobeyed his officer's instructions and did what he could to help her; she and her child survived.

72   (iv.331)   Dr Carmichael took down several versions in South Uist and elsewhere. A young girl who was deeply in love heard it rumoured that because of his mother's persuasion her beloved was going to marry into a richer family. She lost her reason and fled into the hills, where the deer were her companions. When the young man at last found her, she was dying.

76   (ii.159)   From Catrine Mackintosh, cottar, North Uist. The people say that the Virgin made an augury when Jesus was missing, and ascertained that He was in the Temple disputing with the doctors (ii.159). [Luke, 2.]

SOLITARY PRAYER

79   (i. 3)   From Ann MacDonald, crofter's daughter, Lochaber. Old people in the Isles sing this or some other short hymn before prayer. They generally retire to a closet, or an outhouse, to the lee of a knoll, or to the shelter of a dell, that they may not be seen or heard

of men. I have known men and women of
eighty, ninety and a hundred years of age
continue the practice of their lives in going
from one to two miles to the seashore to join
their voices with the voicing of the waves
and their praises with the praises of the
ceaseless sea (1.3).

80   (III.71)   From Little Catherine Macdonald, cottar,
                  Barra.
81, 83, 84 (III.59, 51, 79)   No sources given.
87   (I. 5)   This poem was taken down in 1866 from Mary
                  Macrae, dairy-woman, Harris. She often
                  walked with companions after the work of
                  the day was done distances of ten and fifteen
                  miles to a dance and after dancing all night
                  walked back again to the work of the
                  morning, fresh and vigorous as if nothing
                  unusual had occurred (1.4).

THE FEASTS OF THE YEAR

91   (I.133)   From Angus Gunn, cottar, Lewis.
93   (III.127)   From Mary Maclellan, crofter, Morar.
97   (III.115)   No name is given.
98   (II.274)   Dr Carmichael's note about Easter.
99   (I.183)   From Donald Wilson, crofter, South Uist.
                  Beltane is the first of May (1.182). This is
                  the day of migrating, from townland to
                  moorland, from the winter homestead to the
                  summer sheiling (1.190).
101   (I.193)   From Alexander MacDonald, crofter, Barra.
103   (III. 89)   No source given.
104   (I.195)   From Mor Gillies, cottar, Benbecula.
105   (I.209)   From Janet MacIosaig, crofter's wife, South
                  Uist. *Machair*: sandy plains fringe the
                  Atlantic side of the Outer Isles, closely
                  covered with short green grass, thickly
                  studded with herbs of fragrant odours and
                  plants of lovely hues (II.323).
107   (III.145)   From Ann Livingstone, crofter, Taynuilt.

COLUMBA AND BRIDE

111   (1.163)   From Fionnladh MacCormaig, cowherd, South Uist.

112   (IV. 47)   No name is given.

113   (II. 97)   From Mor MacIosaig, crofter's wife, South Uist.

114   (II.177)   From Janet Campbell, nurse, South Uist. St Brigit's Day is the first of February. Bride is said to preside over fire, over art, over all beauty. Bride is called the aid-woman of Mary and foster-mother of Jesus (1.164ff).

CONCLUSION

117   (II.217)   From John Stewart, merchant, Lismore.